CAMECHIA C. JOHNSON

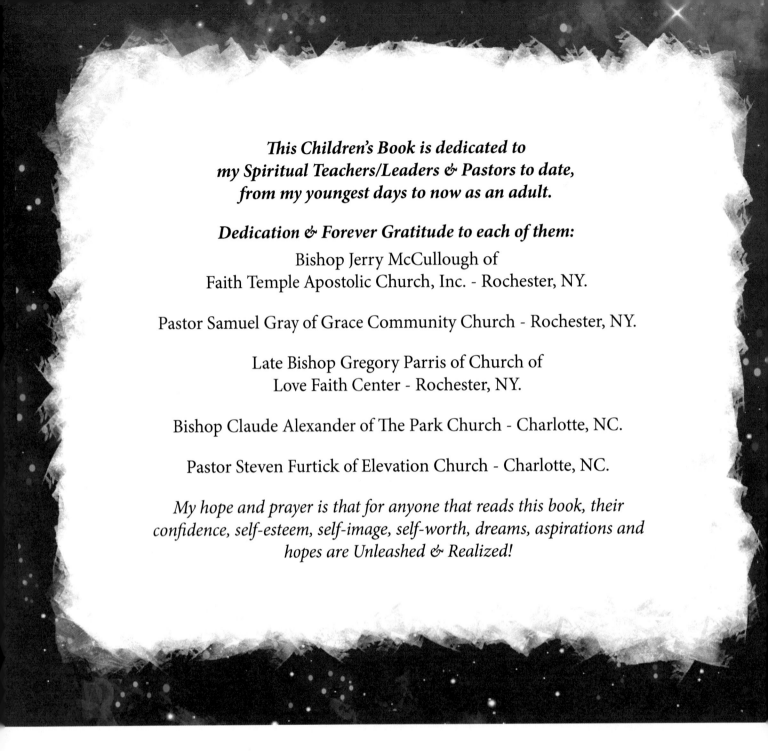

*This Children's Book is dedicated to
my Spiritual Teachers/Leaders & Pastors to date,
from my youngest days to now as an adult.*

Dedication & Forever Gratitude to each of them:

Bishop Jerry McCullough of
Faith Temple Apostolic Church, Inc. - Rochester, NY.

Pastor Samuel Gray of Grace Community Church - Rochester, NY.

Late Bishop Gregory Parris of Church of
Love Faith Center - Rochester, NY.

Bishop Claude Alexander of The Park Church - Charlotte, NC.

Pastor Steven Furtick of Elevation Church - Charlotte, NC.

*My hope and prayer is that for anyone that reads this book, their
confidence, self-esteem, self-image, self-worth, dreams, aspirations and
hopes are Unleashed & Realized!*

Concept Illustrations by Kendra J. Nesmith

Art and Design by Zoe Ranucci, www.gooddharma.com

ISBN: 978-1-5136-8336-2

THIS BOOK
BELONGS TO

_____

Fill in your own affirmation and draw a picture of it!

I AM

_____